YOUR FREE GIFT

I wanted to show my appreciation that you support my work so I've put together a free gift for you.

[Take your Free Bonus here](#)

Just visit the link above to download it now. I know you will love this gift.

Thank you for attention!
With love,
Tommy Jackson

Text Copyright © Tommy Jackson

All rights reserved. No part of this guide may be reproduced in any form without permission in writing from the publisher except in the case of brief quotations embodied in critical articles or reviews.

Legal & Disclaimer

The information contained in this book and its contents is not designed to replace or take the place of any form of medical or professional advice; and is not meant to replace the need for independent medical, financial, legal or other professional advice or services, as may be required. The content and information in this book hasbeen provided for educational and entertainment purposes only.

The content and information contained in this book hasbeen compiled from sources deemed reliable, and it is accurate to the best of the Author's knowledge, information and belief. However, the Author cannot guarantee its accuracy and validity and cannot be held liable for any errors and/or omissions. Further, changes are periodically made to this book as and when needed. Where appropriate and/or necessary, you must consult a professional (including but not limited to your doctor, attorney, financial advisor or such other professional advisor) before using any of the suggested remedies, techniques, or information in this book.

Upon using the contents and information contained in this book, you agree to hold harmless the Author from and against any damages, costs, and expenses, including any legal fees potentially resulting from the application of any of the information provided by this book. This disclaimer applies to any loss, damages or injury caused by the use and application.

Table of Contents

Take your Free Bonus here 1

Introduction 5

Chapter 1: What Does an Air Fryer Do? 6

    Different Types of Air Fryers 6

        Basket Air Fryers 6

        Paddle Air Fryers 7

        Completely Oil Free Fryers 7

    Benefits of Using an Air Fryer 8

        Less Oil 8

        Hands-Free Cooking 8

        Small Appliance, Big Wonders 8

        Easy To Clean 8

        Ideal for Novice Cooks 8

        Saves You Money 9

        Safe To Use 9

Chapter 2: The Recipes 10

    Welsh Rarebit 10

    Breakfast Frittata 12

    Breakfast Sandwich 14

    Homemade Fried Potatoes 16

    Oatmeal Muffins 18

    Cheesy Omelet with Onion 20

    Sausage and Bacon Toast 22

    Sago Galette 24

    Masala Galette 26

    Potato Samosa 28

    Vegetable Kebab 31

    Rosemary Roast Potatoes Air Fryer Style 33

    Baked Macaroni Pasta 35

    Macaroni Samosa 38

- Burritos ...41
- Sweet Potato Fries ...44
- Veg Momos ...46
- Cornflakes French toast ...48
- Freshly Baked Banana Bread ...50
- Cottage Cheese Sticks ...52
- Masala French Fries ...54
- Dal Mint Kebab ...56
- Cottage Cheese Croquette ...59
- Barbeque Corn Sandwich ...62
- Honey Chili Potatoes ...64

Conclusion ...66

Take your Free Bonus here ...67

Introduction

What is an air frying? Air frying has immense benefits. It is great for new cooking experiments with frying, preventing any burns or even fire. The cooling mechanisms and temperature controls within the fryer enable it to protect itself, giving you better tasting food, healthier meals and are environmentally friendly.

How did the AirFryer become so popular? The air fryer was first launched and used in Europe and Australia in 2010. North America and Japan followed soon enough and now it has become a staple in many kitchens. All around the world, people use it to make different dishes according to what is usually eaten in each country. The Japanese use it to make tamagoyaki, gyoza, katsu curries and kaarage. In the UK it is used for chips and fish, sponge cake and croquettes. In India it is used to cook rice and make briyani and samosas whereas in America, people use it to make anything from macaroni and cheese to chicken wings. In the next chapters, we will look into many recipes that you can make in the air fryer to produce healthy and wholesome meals, and not just for deep frying. What are the popular brands of air fryers in the market? Paula Deen Ceramic Air Fryer is popular on the market now.

This fryer is a 3.5-quart fryer that comes with a deep cake pan, steam rack and silicone trivet that enables you to make pizza, cakes, bread and more. Of courses there's also the Nutri Chef Electric Air Fryer that allows you to grill, bake and roast in its 3-quart pan. For a more advanced looking fryer, why not try E'Cucina HealthyFry Air Fryer that comes in a sleek onyx black color with blue LED panels. This fryer ensures an even hot hair circulation even for uneven foods. Plenty of people seem to like Philips XL air fryer because it has a higher cooking time, at 30 percent faster than other competing brands.

The other good thing about the fryer is that it has a bigger cooking capacity, so it can be easily used to cook delicious meals quickly and in larger proportions for big families. Another good one on the list is yet again Philips Viva Collection Air fryer is great for small families and it also has a sleek inlay which means lesser cleaning time. This is ideal for single adults or even students living away from home. Essentially, buy an air fryer that is ideal for your cooking needs and the size of your meals. If you need to cook for a big family, of course opting for XL options is the best but if you need to cook small quantities, then any brand of air fryer can fit your needs because they all have the same cooking abilities, except with new technology to make frying better.

Enjoy.

Chapter 1: What Does an Air Fryer Do?

An air fryer is often referred to as «oil-less fryer» because unlike a deep fat fryer that uses hot oil to fry foods, an air fryer uses the circulation of superheated air to fry foods. The air within the air fryer can heat as high as 392 degrees Fahrenheit. Such high heat allows food to brown, crisp, and cooks through much as the foods would do were they in a traditional deep fat fryer. This hot air is emitted from a heating element in the cooking chamber that is quite close to the food and then an exhaust fan above the food provides circulation for the hot air.

This system lets the superheated air circulate and pass through the food so that it is evenly heated. Since frying technically describes a method of cooking foods in fats and oil, how can an air fryer be considered a fryer? Well, air fryers aren't technically fryers at all. The reason why they are referred to as fryers is that the air fryer was developed to provide a healthy alternative to deep fat frying. In actuality, air fryers are much more like convection oven cooking instead of deep fat fryers. Since companies intended for the air fryer to replace the deep fat fryer, however, marketing teams took to referring to this new cooking method as "air frying."

Different Types of Air Fryers

Technically, there are two different types of air fryers: a basket air fryer and a paddle air fryer. There are, however, a few more categories that can separate some air fryers from others. In this section we will take a look at all of these categories.

Basket Air Fryers

A basket air fryer is a more affordable type of air fryer, but when using this air fryer you may have to stop the fryer multiple times during the cooking process to shake up or turn the food in the fryer to ensure that it is thoroughly cooked. When cooking with a basket air fryer, food needs to be coated with fat before it is put into the cooking basket.

Paddle Air Fryers

A paddle air fryer is usually more expensive air fryer than a basket air fryer, but this expense is justified by the fact that this fryer turns or stirs the food in the fryer while it is cooking. When using the paddle air fryer, fat should be added to the pan with the food before cooking begins.

Completely Oil Free Fryers

Completely oil-free fryers are a favorite among health-conscious people because they don't utilize oils to cook the food. The food from oil free fryers is crisped up simply through the use of hot air circulation as in convection ovens. When people refer to air fryers being similar to convection ovens, this is most often the type of air fryer they are talking about. Without oils, these cookers have absolutely none of the drawbacks of oil fryers. Oil free fryers can be both basket or paddle fryers.

Benefits of Using an Air Fryer

Less Oil

Cook with no oil or very little oil. Either way, you have a low fat and healthy alternative to all kinds of delicious foods. This is great for people losing weight or trying to cut back on fatty and fried foods. With the air fryer, you can have quick, healthy and delicious meals with a touch of a button.

Hands-Free Cooking

You'll be spending a reduced amount of time in the kitchen and have more time to do other things like reply emails or watch TV or spend time with your spouse and kids while the air fryer is cooking your meals. All you need to do is a put a few things together, place them in your air fryer and leave. The beeper will tell you when it's done.

Small Appliance, Big Wonders

You can fry, you can bake, you can sauté in this little air fryer. It is a great device to have in a small kitchen and especially convenient if you are sharing a dorm or renting an apartment.

Easy To Clean

Especially for busy moms and dads, this air fryer lessens even more time over the sink because there's not much to clean. Make frying or baking even more convenient by covering the fryer basket with aluminum foil or baking paper.

Ideal for Novice Cooks

New to the kitchen? With the air fryer, making gourmet meals, frying fish, chicken or even fries is easy and convenient. The air fryer helps the novice cook to learn the basics of cooking but without all the fuss and that comes with wok frying or stove cooking.

Saves You Money

With less oil usage with the air fryer, this means you spend less on cooking oil. The air fryer is also energy efficient which means you do not rake up high electricity bills. The fact that it uses less oil also means that you can now buy organic gourmet oils to enhance the flavors of your food since you only need the bare minimum.

Safe To Use

With the air fryer, say goodbye to oil spills, smoky kitchen and oil splatters. The air fryer enables you to 'deep fry' foods without the mess and possibility of getting scalded by hot oil. Anyone can use the air fryer for single adults, busy moms, busy dads, teenagers and students living away from home. You can whip up delicious meals quickly and easily without worrying about getting the room clogged with fried oil and smoke, oil stains. The air fryer is safe and easy to use.

Chapter 2: The Recipes

Welsh Rarebit

Serves: 2

Prep time: 10 mins

Cook time: 15 mins

Ingredients:

- *•3 bread slices*
- *•2 large eggs (separated)*
- *•1 tsp. of mustard*
- *•1 tsp. of paprika*
- *•120g of Cheddar*

Directions:

1. Very lightly heat up 3 bread slices in your Air Fryer so that it is almost like toast. The best way to do this is to give it 5 minutes at 356 °F.

2. Whisk the egg whites in a bowl until they form soft peaks.

3. Mix the egg yolks, cheese, paprika and mustard in a bowl.

4. Then fold in the egg whites.

5. Spoon it onto the partly toasted bread and cook in the Air Fryer for 10 minutes at 356 °F.

6. Serve!

Breakfast Frittata

Preparation time: 5 minutes

Cooking time: 10 minutes

Servings: 4

Ingredients:

- *½ Italian sausage*
- *3 eggs*
- *4 cherry tomatoes, cut in half*

- *1 tbsp. of olive oil*

- *Parsley, chopped*

- *Parmesan cheese*

- *Pepper*

- *Salt*

Directions:

1. Preheat your Air Fryer to 360°F.

2. Place tomatoes and sausage in a lined baking sheet. Place in the Air Fryer and bake for 5 minutes at 360°F.

3. Whisk the remaining ingredients together in a small bowl.

4. Remove baked tomatoes and sausages from the Air Fryer. Add the mixture evenly; return to the Air Fryer and bake for another 5 minutes.

Breakfast Sandwich

Preparation time: 4 minutes

Cooking time: 6 minutes

Servings: 2

Ingredients:

- *1 free range egg*
- *1 English muffin*
- *2 streaky bacons or 1 English bacon*
- *1 pinch of pepper*
- *1 pinch of salt*

Directions:

1. Break egg into an oven proof bowl or soufflé cup.

2. Add 1 muffin and bacon, and then place into your Air Fryer.

3. Cook for 6 minutes at 395°F.

4. Arrange sandwich and serve. Enjoy

Homemade Fried Potatoes

Preparation time: 30 minutes

Cooking time: 35 minutes

Servings: 4

Ingredients:

- *3 large-sized potatoes, scrubbed and chopped into ½ - ¾ cubes*
- *1 medium size onion, finely chopped*
- *2 tbsp. of bacon grease (or olive oil, Ghee or Coconut oil)*
- *2 tsp. of smoked salt (or sea salt)*
- *1 tsp. of powdered garlic*
- *1 tsp. of powdered Onion*
- *1 tsp. of Paprika*
- *1 small red pepper, diced (optional)*

Directions:

1. Put potatoes into a strainer, and then place in a large bowl. Cover with water and soak for 20 to 30 minutes.

2. While the potatoes are soaking, chop red pepper and onions.

3. Combine all the seasonings.

4. Drain the potatoes and dry properly, and then put into a large mixing bowl.

5. Add the diced peppers, onions and bacon grease and mix together properly.

6. Pour the potato mixture into an Air Fryer bowl or basket and cook for 25 to 30 minutes at 380°F. Shake the basket when the potatoes are halfway through. Add more time if required, the potatoes should be soft by this time.

7. Transfer the cooked potato mixture to a large mixing bowl; add seasonings and mix properly.

8. Return to the Air fryer and cook for 5 minutes at 380°F.

Oatmeal Muffins

Preparation time: 5 minutes

Cooking time: 15 minutes

Servings: 2-4

Ingredients

- *2 eggs*
- *3½ ounces of oats*
- *3-ounces of melted butter*
- *1/2 cup of flour*
- *1/4 teaspoon of vanilla essence*

- *1/2 cup of icing sugar*

- *A pinch of baking powder*

- *1 tablespoon of raisins*

- *Cooking spray*

Directions:

1. Combine sugar and butter until they are soft. Whisk together 2 eggs and vanilla essence. Add it to the sugar/butter mix until soft peaks forms.

2. Combine flour, raisins, baking powder and oats in a separate bowl. Add it to the mixed ingredients.

3. Grease the muffin tins lightly with cooking spray and fill with the batter mixture. Preheat your Air Fryer at 350°F.

4. Place the muffin tins into the air fryer tray. Let it cook for 12 minutes. Cool, serve and enjoy!

Cheesy Omelet with Onion

Preparation time: 5 minutes

Cooking time: 15 minutes

Servings: 2

Ingredients:

- *2 eggs*
- *1 medium onion, sliced*
- *Soy Sauce*
- *Grated cheddar cheese*
- *Pepper*
- *Cooking spray*

Directions:

1. Beat eggs in a bowl and season with pepper and soy sauce.

2. Grease a pan (one that fits properly into the Air Fryer) with cooking spray.

3. Put sliced onions into the greased pan and fry at 356°F for 8 to 10 minutes or until they are softened.

4. Pour the egg mixture into the pan; sprinkle grated Cheddar cheese over top and continue frying for another 3-5 minutes or until it is properly cooked.

Sausage and Bacon Toast

Preparation time: 2 minutes

Cooking time: 20 minutes

Servings: 4

Ingredients:

- *8 medium size sausages*
- *8 Rashers, non-smoked back bacon*
- *4 eggs*
- *1 can baked beans*
- *8 toast slices*

Directions:

1. Place 8 sausages and bacon in the Air Fryer and cook at 320°F for 10 minutes.

2. Place all baked beans in a ramekin and place the prepared (ready to be fried) egg in another ramekin.

3. Cook for another 10 minutes at 392°F or until everything is well cooked.

4. Serve and enjoy.

Cooking tips:

Add hash browns, black pudding or fried mushroom if desired. You may replace toast with fried bread if desired.

Sago Galette

Preparation time: 5 minutes

Cooking time: 30 minutes

Servings: 4

Ingredients:

- *2 cups of sago soaked*
- *1 ½ cups of coarsely crushed peanuts*
- *3 tsp. of ginger, finely chopped*
- *1-2 tbsp. of fresh coriander leaves*
- *2 or 3 green chilies, finely chopped*
- *1 ½ tbsp. of lemon juice*
- *Salt, pepper*

Directions:

Wash all soaked sago and mix it with the other ingredients in a clean bowl.

Mold this mixture into round and flat galettes.

Wet the galettes slightly with water. Coat each galette with crushed peanuts.

Preheat your Air Fryer at 160 degrees F for 5 minutes. Place the galettes in the fry basket and let them cook for another 25 minutes at the same temperature.

Serve either with mint chutney or ketchup.

Masala Galette

Preparation time: 8 minutes

Cooking time: 25 minutes

Servings: 4

Ingredients:

- •2 tbsp. of garam masala

- •2 medium potatoes, boiled and mashed

- •1 ½ cups of coarsely crushed peanuts

- •3 tsp. of ginger, finely chopped

- •1-2 tbsp. of fresh coriander leaves

- •2 or 3 green chilies, finely chopped

- •1 ½ tbsp. of lemon juice

- •Salt and pepper

Directions:

Mix all the ingredients in a clean bowl.

Mold this mixture into round and flat galettes.

Wet the galettes slightly with water.

Coat each galette with crushed peanuts.

Preheat your Air Fryer to 160 degrees Fahrenheit for 5 minutes.

Place the galettes in the fry basket and let them cook for another 20 minutes at the same temperature.

Serve either with mint chutney or ketchup.

Potato Samosa

Preparation time: 10 minutes

Cooking time: 40 minutes

Servings: 3

Ingredients:

For wrappers:

- •2 tbsp. of unsalted butter
- •1 ½ cups of all-purpose flour
- •A pinch of salt to taste
- •Add as much water as required to make the dough stiff and firm

For filling:

- *•2-3 big potatoes, boiled and mashed*
- *•¼ cup of boiled peas*
- *•1 tsp. of powdered ginger*
- *•1-2 green chilies, finely chopped or mashed*
- *•½ tsp. of cumin*
- *•1 tsp. of coarsely crushed coriander*
- *•1 dry red chili, broken into pieces*
- *•A small amount of salt (to taste)*
- *•½ tsp. of dried mango powder*
- *•½ tsp. of red chili power*
- *•1-2 tbsp. of coriander*

Directions:

Mix the dough for the outer covering and make it stiff and smooth. Leave it to rest in a container while making the filling.

Cook the ingredients in a pan and stir them well to make a thick paste. Roll the paste out.

Roll the dough into balls and flatten them. Cut them into halves and add the filling. Use water to help you fold the edges to create the shape of a cone.

Preheat your Air Fryer for 5-6 minutes at 300 F.

Place all the samosas in the fry basket and close the basket properly.

Keep the Air Fryer at 200 degrees for another 20 to 25 minutes.

After this, fry at 250 degrees for 10 minutes in order to give them the desired golden brown color.

Serve hot. Recommended sides are tamarind or mint chutney.

Vegetable Kebab

Preparation time: 5 minutes

Cooking time: 30 minutes

Servings: 5

Ingredients:

- •2 cups of mixed vegetables
- •3 onions, chopped
- •5 green chilies-roughly chopped
- •1 ½ tbsp. of ginger paste
- •1 ½ tsp. of garlic paste
- •1 ½ tsp. of salt

- •3 tsp. of lemon juice
- •2 tsp. of garam masala
- •4 tbsp. of chopped coriander
- •3 tbsp. of cream
- •3 tbsp. of chopped capsicum
- •3 eggs
- •2 ½ tbsp. of white sesame seeds

Directions:

Grind the ingredients except for eggs and form a smooth paste.

Coat the vegetables in the paste.

Now, beat the eggs and add some salt to it.

Dip the coated vegetables in the egg mixture and then transfer to sesame seeds and coat the vegetables well.

Place the vegetables on a stick.

Preheat your Air fryer at 160 degrees F for 5 minutes.

Place the sticks in the basket and let them cook for another 25 minutes at the same temperature.

Turn the sticks over.

Rosemary Roast Potatoes Air Fryer Style

Preparation time: 5 minutes

Cooking time: 10 minutes

Servings: 5

Ingredients:

- *•2 Large Potatoes*
- *•1 tsp. of Rosemary*
- *•1 tbsp. of Olive Oil*
- *•Salt & Pepper*

Directions:

1. Peel potatoes and cut them into roast potato shapes.

2. Place them in your Air Fryer for 10 minutes at 356 °F temperature with 1 tablespoon of olive oil.

3. When cooked place them in a mixing bowl and sprinkle with rosemary, salt and pepper.

4. Mix well and then serve.

Baked Macaroni Pasta

Preparation time: 5 minutes

Cooking time: 15 minutes

Servings: 4

Ingredients:

- *•1 cup of pasta*
- *•7 cups of boiling water*
- *•1 ½ tbsp. of olive oil*
- *•A pinch of salt*
- *For tossing pasta:*

- •1 ½ tbsp. of olive oil
- •½ cup of carrot small pieces
- •Salt and pepper
- •½ tsp. of oregano
- •½ tsp. of basil
- For white sauce:
- •2 tbsp. of olive oil
- •2 tbsp. of all-purpose flour
- •2 cups of milk
- •1 tsp. of dried oregano
- •½ tsp. of dried basil
- •½ tsp. of dried parsley
- •Salt and pepper

Directions:

Cook the pasta. You will need to toss the pasta in the ingredients mentioned above and set aside.

For the sauce, add all the ingredients to a pan and bring them to a boil.

Stir the sauce and continue to simmer to make a thicker sauce.

Add the pasta to the sauce and transfer this into a glass bowl garnished with cheese.

Preheat your Air Fryer at 160 degrees C for 5 minutes.

Place the bowl in the basket and close it.

Let it continue to cook at the same temperature for 10 minutes.

Keep stirring the pasta.

Macaroni Samosa

Preparation time: 5 minutes

Cooking time: 46 minutes

Servings: 2

Ingredients:

- *For wrappers*:
- •1 cup of all-purpose flour
- •2 tbsp. of unsalted butter
- •A pinch of salt to taste

- •Take the amount of water sufficient enough to make stiff dough

For filling:

- •3 cups of boiled macaroni
- •2 onions, sliced
- •2 capsicums, sliced
- •2 carrots, sliced
- •2 cabbages, sliced
- •2 tbsp. of soya sauce
- •2 tsp. of vinegar
- •2 tbsp. of ginger, finely chopped
- •2 tbsp. of garlic, finely chopped
- •2 tbsp. of green, chilies finely chopped
- •2 tbsp. of ginger-garlic paste
- •Salt and pepper
- •2 tbsp. of olive oil
- •½ tsp. of ajinomoto

Directions:

Mix the dough for the outer covering and make it stiff and smooth. Leave it to rest in a container while making the filling.

Cook all the ingredients in a pan and stir them well to make a thick paste.

Roll the paste out.

Roll the dough into balls and flatten them.

Cut them in halves and add the filling. Use water to help you fold the edges to create the shape of a cone.

Pre-heat your Air Fryer for 6 minutes at 300 F.

Place all the samosas in the fry basket and close the basket properly.

Keep the Air Fryer at 200 degrees for another 20 minutes.

After this, fry at 250 degrees for 10 minutes in order to give them the desired golden brown color.

Serve hot.

Burritos

Preparation time: 10 minutes

Cooking time: 25 minutes

Servings: 2

Ingredients:

Refried beans:

- •½ cup of red kidney beans (soaked overnight)
- •½ small onion, chopped
- •1 tbsp. of olive oil
- •2 tbsp. of tomato puree
- •¼ tsp. of red chili powder

- •1 tsp. of salt to taste
- •4-5 flour tortillas

Vegetable Filling:

- •1 tbsp. of Olive oil
- •1 medium onion, finely sliced
- •3 garlic cloves, crushed
- •½ cup **of French** beans (Slice them lengthwise into thin and long slices)
- •½ cup of mushrooms, thinly sliced
- •1 cup of cottage cheese cut into long and slightly thick fingers
- •½ cup of shredded cabbage
- •1 tbsp. of coriander, chopped
- •1 tbsp. of vinegar
- •1 tsp. of white wine
- •A pinch of salt to taste
- •½ tsp. of red chili flakes
- •1 tsp. of freshly ground peppercorns
- •½ cup of pickled jalapenos (Chop them up finely)
- •2 carrots (Cut in to long thin slices)

- *Salad:*
- •1-2 lettuce leaves, shredded.
- •1 or 2 spring onions, chopped finely. Also cut the greens.
- •1 tomato, remove the seeds and chop it into small pieces.
- •1 green chili chopped.
- •1 cup of cheddar cheese, grated.

Directions:

Cook beans with onion and garlic and mash them finely.

Now, make the sauce you will need for the burrito. Ensure that you create a slightly thick sauce.

For the filling, you will need to cook the ingredients well in a pan and make ensure that the vegetables have browned on the outside.

To make the salad, toss the ingredients together.

Place the tortilla and add a layer of sauce, followed by the beans and the filling at the center. Before you roll it, you will need to place the salad on top of the filling.

Pre-heat the Air Fryer for around 5 minutes at 200 Fahrenheit.

Open the fry basket and keep the burritos inside. Close the basket properly.

Let the Air Fryer stay at 200 Fahrenheit for another 15 minutes or so.

Serve and enjoy.

Sweet Potato Fries

Serves: 2

Prep time: 5 mins

Cook time: 20 mins

Ingredients:

- •300g sweet potatoes
- •3 tbsp. of olive oil
- •1 tsp. of Mustard Powder
- •Salt & Pepper

Directions:

1. Peel and chop up all sweet potatoes so that they resemble chunky chips.

2. Place them in your Air fryer with 2 tablespoons of olive oil and shake them so

that the sweet potatoes are well covered.

3. Cook for 15 minutes at 180c. Though at the halfway mark give the sweet

potatoes a shake so that none are getting stuck to the bottom and so that they

are all getting the effect of the olive oil.

4. When cooked remove them from the air fryer and place them in a bowl. Add

the last tablespoon of olive oil with the seasoning and mix well. ′

5. Serve.

Veg Momos

Preparation time: 8 minutes

Cooking time: 25 minutes

Servings: 3

Ingredients:

For dough:

- •1 ½ cups of all-purpose flour
- •½ tsp. of salt or to taste
- •5 tbsp. of water

For filling:

- •2 cups of carrots grated
- •2 cups of cabbage grated
- •2 tbsp. of oil
- •2 tsp. of ginger-garlic paste
- •2 tsp. of soya sauce
- •2 tsp. of vinegar

Directions:

Knead the dough and cover it with plastic wrap and set aside.

Next, cook the ingredients for the filling and try to make sure that the vegetables are covered well with the sauce.

Roll the dough and cut it into squares.

Place the filling in the center. Now, wrap the dough to cover the filling and pinch the edges together.

Preheat the Air fryer at 200° F for 5 minutes.

Place the gnocchi's in the fry basket and close it. Let them cook at the same temperature for another 20 minutes.

Grease the dish with chili sauce or ketchup.

Cornflakes French toast

Preparation time: 6 minutes

Cooking time: 25 minutes

Servings: 3

Ingredients:

- •Bread slices (brown or white)
- •1 egg white for 2 slices
- •1 tsp. of sugar for 2 slices
- •Crushed cornflakes

Directions:

Put two slices together and cut them along the diagonal.

In a bowl, whisk the egg whites and add some sugar.

Dip the bread triangles into this mixture and then coat them with the crushed cornflakes.

Preheat your Air Fryer at 180° C for 4 minutes.

Place the coated bread triangles in the fry basket and close it.

Let them cook at the same temperature for another 20 minutes at least.

Serve these slices with chocolate sauce.

Freshly Baked Banana Bread

Preparation time: 10 minutes

Cooking time: 30 minutes

Servings: 4

Ingredients:

- •225g of self-raising flour
- •¼ tsp. of Bicarbonate of Soda
- •75g of Butter

- •175g Caster Sugar
- •2 medium eggs
- •450g Bananas (weight with peeling)
- •100g chopped walnuts

Directions:

1. Preheat the air fryer to 356 °F.

2. Grease a tin that will slot into your air fryer.

3. Mix together bicarbonate of soda with flour.

4. In a separate bowl cream butter and sugar until fluffy, then add eggs a little at a time with a little flour with each.

5. Stir in the remaining flour and walnuts.

6. Peel bananas and mash them up and also add them to your mixture.

7. Place the banana bread mix into the tin and cook for 10 minutes at 356 °F

8. Serve!

Cottage Cheese Sticks

Preparation time: 5 minutes

Cooking time: 35 minutes

Servings: 2

Ingredients:

- •2 cups of cottage cheese
- •1 big lemon-juiced
- •1 tbsp. of ginger-garlic paste
- •For seasoning, use salt and red chili powder in small amounts
- •½ tsp. of carom
- •1-2 papadums
- •4 or 5 tbsp. of corn flour

- •1 cup of water

Directions:

Cut cottage cheese into long pieces.

Now, make a mixture of lemon juice, red chili powder, salt, ginger garlic paste and carom to use as a marinade.

Let the cottage cheese pieces marinate in the mixture for some time and then roll them in dry corn flour.

Leave them aside for 20 minutes.

Put papadums into a pan and roast them. Once they are cooked, crush them into very small pieces.

Now, take another container and pour around 100 ml of water into it.

Dissolve 2 tbsp. of corn flour in this water.

Dip the cottage cheese pieces in this solution of corn flour and roll them on to the pieces of crushed papadum so that the papadum sticks to the cottage cheese.

Preheat your Air Fryer for 10 minutes at 290 Fahrenheit.

Then open the basket of the fryer and place the cottage cheese pieces inside it.

Close the basket properly. Let the fryer stay at 160 degrees for another 20 minutes.

When they are done, you can serve it either with ketchup or mint chutney.

Masala French Fries

Preparation time: 8 minutes

Cooking time: 30 minutes

Servings: 2

Ingredients:

- •2 medium sized potatoes, peeled and cut into thick pieces lengthwise
- *Ingredients for the marinade:*
- •1 tbsp. of olive oil
- •1 tsp. of mixed herbs
- •½ tsp. of red chili flakes
- •A pinch of salt to taste
- •1 tbsp. of lemon juice

Directions:

Boil potatoes and blanch them.

Cut the potatoes into thick pieces.

Mix all the ingredients for the marinade and add the potatoes to it making sure that they are coated well.

Preheat your Air Fryer for 5 minutes at 300 F.

Take out the basket of the fryer and place the potatoes into it.

Close the basket.

Now, keep the fryer at 200 F for 20-25 minutes.

During the process, toss the fries twice so that they get cooked properly.

Dal Mint Kebab

Preparation time: 10 minutes

Cooking time: 35 minutes

Servings: 2

Ingredients:

- •1 cup of chickpeas
- •Half ginger, grated or 1 tsp. of ginger-garlic paste
- •1-2 green chilies, chopped finely
- •¼ tsp. of red chili powder
- •A pinch of salt to taste

- •½ tsp. of roasted cumin powder
- •2 tsp. of coriander powder
- •1 ½ tbsp. of chopped coriander
- •½ tsp. of dried mango powder
- •1 cup of dry breadcrumbs
- •¼ tsp. of black salt
- •1-2 tbsp. of all-purpose flour for coating purposes
- •1-2 tbsp. of mint (finely chopped)
- •1 onion, finely chopped
- •½ cup of milk

Directions:

Take an open vessel. Boil the chickpeas in the vessel until their texture becomes soft. Make sure that they do not become soggy.

Now put chickpeas into another container.

Add grated ginger and cut green chilies.

Grind this mixture until it becomes a thick paste.

Keep adding water as and when required.

Now add onions, mint, and bread-crumbs.

Mix this well until you get a soft dough.

Now take small balls of this mixture (about the size of a lemon) and mold them into the shape of flat and round kebabs.

Here is where the milk comes into play.

Pour a very small amount of milk onto each kebab to wet it. Now roll the kebab in the dry breadcrumbs.

Preheat your Air Fryer for 5 minutes at 300 F.

Take out the basket.

Arrange the kebabs in the basket leaving gaps between them so that no two kebabs are touching each other.

Keep the fryer at 340 F for half an hour.

Half way through the cooking process, turn the kebabs over so that they can be cooked properly.

Grease the dish with mint chutney, tomato ketchup or yoghurt chutney.

Cottage Cheese Croquette

Preparation time: 5 minutes

Cooking time: 20 minutes

Servings: 2

Ingredients:

- •2 cups of cottage cheese, cut into long pieces
- •1 big capsicum
- •1 onion
- •5 tbsp. of gram flour
- •A pinch of salt to taste

For chutney:

- •2 cups of fresh green coriander
- •½ cup of mint leaves
- •4 tsp. of fennel
- •1 small onion
- •2 tbsp. of ginger-garlic paste
- •6-7 garlic flakes (optional)
- •3 tbsp. of lemon juice
- •Salt

Directions:

Take a clean and dry container.

Put into it the coriander: mint, fennel, and ginger, onion/garlic, salt and lemon juice.

Mix them. Pour the mixture into a grinder and blend until you get a thick paste.

Now move on to the cottage cheese pieces.

Slit these pieces almost till the end and leave them aside.

Stuff all the pieces with the paste that was obtained from the previous step.

Leave the stuffed cottage cheese aside.

Take the chutney and add to it the gram flour and some salt.

Mix them together properly. Rub this mixture all over the stuffed cottage cheese pieces.

Now, to the leftover chutney, add capsicum and onions.

Apply the chutney generously on the pieces of capsicum and onion.

Now take satay sticks and arrange the cottage cheese pieces and vegetables on separate sticks.

Preheat your Air Fryer at 290 F for 5 minutes.

Open the basket. Arrange the satay sticks properly.

Keep the sticks with the cottage cheese at 180 degrees C for half an hour while the sticks with the vegetables are kept at the same temperature for only 7 minutes.

Barbeque Corn Sandwich

Preparation time: 5 minutes

Cooking time: 20 minutes

Servings: 3

Ingredients:

- •2 slices of white bread
- •1 tbsp. of softened butter
- •1 cup of sweet corn kernels
- •1 small capsicum

For Barbeque Sauce:

- •¼ tbsp. of Worcestershire sauce
- •½ tsp. of olive oil
- •½ flake garlic crushed
- •¼ cup of chopped onion
- •¼ tbsp. of red chili sauce
- •½ cup of water

Directions:

Take the slices of bread and remove the edges. Now cut the slices horizontally.

Cook the ingredients for the sauce and wait until they are thickened.

Now, add the corn to the sauce and stir till it obtains the flavors.

Roast the capsicum and peel the skin off.

Cut the capsicum into slices. Apply the sauce to the slices.

Preheat your Air Fryer for 5 minutes at 300 F.

Open the basket of the Fryer and place the prepared sandwiches in it such that no two sandwiches are touching each other.

Now keep the fryer at 250 degrees for 15 minutes. Turn the sandwiches during the cooking process to cook both slices. Serve the sandwiches with tomato ketchup or mint chutney.

Honey Chili Potatoes

Preparation time: 5 minutes

Cooking time: 25 minutes

Servings: 2

Ingredients:

For potato:

- •3 big potatoes (Cut into strips or cubes)
- •2 ½ tsp. of ginger-garlic paste
- •¼ tsp. of salt
- •1 tsp. of red chili sauce
- •¼ tsp. of red chili powder/black pepper
- •A few drops of edible orange food coloring

For sauce:

- •1 capsicum, cut into thin and long pieces (lengthwise).
- •2 tbsp. of olive oil
- •2 onions, cut into halves.
- •1 ½ tbsp. of sweet chili sauce
- •1 ½ tsp. of ginger garlic paste
- •½ tbsp. of red chili sauce
- •2 tbsp. of tomato ketchup
- •2 tsp. of soya sauce
- •2 tsp. of vinegar
- •A pinch of black pepper powder
- •1-2 tsp. of red chili flakes

Directions:

Create the mix for the potatoes and coat the chicken well with it.

Preheat your Air fryer at 250 F for 5 minutes.

Open the basket of the Fryer.

Place the potatoes into the basket.

Cook at 290 F for 20 minutes.

Conclusion

Air fryers are a healthy alternative to cooking your previously deep-fried favorites. By using minimal amounts of oil, the same dish can have a significantly lower fat content when made in an air fryer rather than traditionally. But what recipes are best for your air frying adventures? To answer that, we made a compilation of our favorite air fryer appetizer, dessert, and classic fried potato recipes for you to try out.

One of the greatest benefits is the ability to cook with little or no oil. If you want to minimize or eliminate oily foods from your diet, this is the appliance for you. Now you can have low-fat versions of favorite foods like French fries and fried chicken. You can have healthy versions of the meals you love without compromising on taste.

An air fryer is a multipurpose appliance that provides you with a variety of cooking options. It can be used to fry, grill, bake or roast ingredients. It can cook more than one dish at once thereby saving time. It has easily removable parts for easy cleaning.

YOUR FREE GIFT

I wanted to show my appreciation that you support my work so I've put together a free gift for you.

Take your Free Bonus here

Just visit the link above to download it now. I know you will love this gift.

Thank you for attention!
With love,
Tommy Jackson

Made in the USA
Middletown, DE
12 December 2020